CLEOPATRA

The woman behind the stories

ALEXANDRA STEWART

Illustrated by
HANNAH PECK

BLOOMSBURY
CHILDREN'S BOOKS
LONDON OXFORD NEW YORK NEW DELHI SYDNEY

CHARACTERS YOU WILL MEET IN THIS BOOK

Alexander the Great (356 BCE – 323 BCE) was a powerful Macedonian ruler. One of history's greatest military minds, he created the largest empire in the ancient world.

Ptolemy I (367 BCE – 282 BCE) was one of Alexander the Great's generals. He ruled Egypt after Alexander died and founded the Ptolemaic dynasty.

Ptolemy XII Auletes (Approx. 112 BCE – 51 BCE) was Cleopatra's father. He ruled Egypt from 80 BCE until his death.

Cleopatra VII (69 BCE – 30 BCE) was the last pharaoh of Egypt and the hero of our story.

Berenice IV (77 BCE – 55 BCE) was the eldest daughter of Ptolemy XII. She proclaimed herself ruler of Egypt when her father fled to Rome in 58 BCE, but on his return he executed her.

Arsinoe IV (63 BCE – 41 BCE) was the youngest daughter of Ptolemy XII. She tried to lead Egyptian forces against Cleopatra and Julius Caesar in the Alexandrian War. She became a Roman prisoner until Mark Antony executed her.

Ptolemy XIII (62 BCE – 47 BCE) was the son of Ptolemy XII. He became co-ruler of Egypt with Cleopatra after their father's death. He was killed while leading the Ptolemaic army against Julius Caesar's forces in the Alexandrian War.

Ptolemy XIV Philopator (59 BCE – 44 BCE) was the son of Ptolemy XII. He co-ruled Egypt with Cleopatra after Ptolemy XIII was killed. His own death was mysterious, most probably caused by Cleopatra.

Pothinus (Unknown – 48 BCE) was Ptolemy XIII's scheming advisor. He was executed for turning Ptolemy against Cleopatra and causing the Alexandrian War.

Gnaeus Pompeius Magnus a.k.a Pompey the Great (106 BCE – 48 BCE) was a Roman general, politician and Julius Caesar's rival. Ptolemy XIII ordered his murder after being advised by Pothinus.

Julius Caesar (100 BCE – 44 BCE) was a Roman general, politician and dictator of Rome. He married Cleopatra in an Egyptian ceremony and they had a baby. A group of Roman senators (politicians) assassinated him.

Apollodorus the Sicilian (Dates unknown) was the trusted servant who smuggled Cleopatra into the Royal Palace in Alexandria to meet Julius Caesar for the first time.

Gaius Cassius Longinus (86 BCE – 42 BCE) and Marcus Junius Brutus (85 BCE – 42 BCE) were Roman politicians who spearheaded the plot to assassinate Julius Caesar.

Mark Antony (83 BCE – 30 BCE) was a Roman general, Julius Caesar's trusted advisor and Octavian's rival for leadership of Rome. He married Cleopatra after Caesar's death and they had three children.

Octavian (63 BCE – 14 CE) was Julius Caesar's nephew and heir, and Mark Antony's rival for leading Rome. His troops beat Antony and Cleopatra at the Battle of Actium and he became the first emperor of Rome (renaming himself Caesar Augustus).

Marcus Lepidus (89 BCE – 12 BCE) was a Roman general and politician who briefly ruled the Roman Empire alongside Octavian and Mark Antony in a three-way pact known as the 'Triumvirate'.

Octavia the Younger (69 BCE – 11 BCE) was Octavian's older sister, and Mark Antony's fourth wife before he married Cleopatra.

Ptolemy Caesar (17 BCE – 30 BCE) was Cleopatra's first son and heir. Fathered by Julius Caesar, he was nicknamed Caesarion, meaning 'little Caesar'.

Cleopatra Selene II (40 BCE – approx. 5 BCE) and Alexander Helios (40 BCE – approx. 29 BCE) were Cleopatra's first children with Mark Antony.

Ptolemy Philadelphus (36 BCE – approx. 29 BCE) was Cleopatra's fourth child, her third with Mark Antony. It's likely he died shortly after Cleopatra's death.

King Artavasdes II of Armenia (Unknown – 31 BCE) deserted the Roman forces, led by Mark Antony, in the fight against Parthia. He was captured by Mark Antony and paraded with his family through the streets of Alexandria in silver chains.

Agrippa (63 BCE – 12 BCE) was the talented Roman admiral who led Octavian's fleet against Cleopatra's fleet at the Battle of Actium.

Charmion and Eiras (Unknown – 30 BCE) were Cleopatra's maids. They died alongside her.

For my daughter, Flora. – A.S.

For Will. Give me back my legions. – H.P.

BLOOMSBURY CHILDREN'S BOOKS
Bloomsbury Publishing Plc
50 Bedford Square, London, WC1B 3DP, UK
29 Earlsfort Terrace, Dublin 2, Ireland

BLOOMSBURY, BLOOMSBURY CHILDREN'S BOOKS and the Diana logo are trademarks of Bloomsbury Publishing Plc

First published in Great Britain in 2024 by Bloomsbury Publishing Plc

Text copyright © Alexandra Stewart, 2024
Illustrations copyright © Hannah Peck, 2024
With special thanks to Professor Joann Fletcher for her consultancy

Alexandra Stewart and Hannah Peck have asserted their right under the Copyright, Designs and Patents Act, 1988,
to be identified as Author and Illustrator of this work

All rights reserved.
No part of this publication may be reproduced or transmitted in any form or by any means, electronic or mechanical, including photocopying, recording, or any information storage or retrieval system, without prior permission in writing from the publishers

A catalogue record for this book is available from the British Library

ISBN: HB: 978-1-5266-1903-7 ; eBook: 978-1-5266-6814-1; audio: 978-1-5266-6813-4
2 4 6 8 10 9 7 5 3 1

Printed in China at Golden Prosperity Printing and Packaging (Huizhou) Co. Ltd, HuiZhou City, Guangdong

To find out more about our authors and books visit www.bloomsbury.com and sign up for our newsletters

AUTHOR'S NOTE: THE MANY FACES OF CLEOPATRA

We can all picture Cleopatra's face, can't we? Raven-haired and radiantly beautiful – she has gone down in legend as one of the most handsome women who ever lived. But did you know that nobody can say for sure what Cleopatra really looked like? For a start, there are no first-hand descriptions or paintings of her. And, although she appears in ancient Egyptian wall carvings, this type of symbolic art was never meant to be realistic. In fact, the only contemporary portraits we have of Cleopatra – the portraits which were created while she was alive – are on coins minted during her reign. But these unflattering pictures were designed to advertise Cleopatra's power, rather than show people exactly what she looked like.

History hasn't left us completely in the dark though. One fresco (wall painting), found in an ancient Roman villa, throws some light on this powerful pharaoh's true features. Painted after Cleopatra's death, it shows a lady with reddish-brown hair, lightly tanned skin and a long nose. Whilst this is worlds away from the Cleopatra we've come to know, many historians think that this flame-haired lady could, in fact, be the real Cleopatra. One such historian is the renowned Egyptologist Joann Fletcher. Joann has been scouring the sources and carefully examining the evidence for almost forty years and, for this reason, we have chosen to base our illustrations of Cleopatra on her expert advice, which can also be found in her book *Cleopatra the Great: the Woman Behind the Legend*.

Putting all the uncertainties about Cleopatra's looks aside though, what we can say for sure is that she carefully controlled her image. Just like a chameleon, Cleopatra cleverly changed her appearance to suit every occasion. So, when she presented herself to her Egyptian subjects, she dressed as the mighty Egyptian goddess Isis. When she wanted to impress someone special, she had other dazzling tricks up her sleeves (as you'll discover on page 42). And in private, just like royalty today, Cleopatra would swap her fancy costumes for something more comfortable. As you read through the book and look at the pictures, you'll see the famous pharaoh in all of these guises!

But although time and Cleopatra's chameleon ways have obscured her real face, discussions about what she truly looked like are actually a bit of a distraction. This is why I wanted to make this note before diving headlong into Cleopatra's story. Because, when it comes to understanding the real Cleopatra, what really matters is not what she looked like, but her character. Above all else, it was Cleopatra's razor-sharp mind, sparkling charm and unshakeable self-belief that made her who she was. It was these qualities that equipped her to become one of the most powerful and impressive rulers of her age. And it was how she used these qualities that makes her story so exciting, and so extraordinary ... as you are about to find out for yourself!

I hope you enjoy meeting Cleopatra as much as I did!

Alexandra Stewart

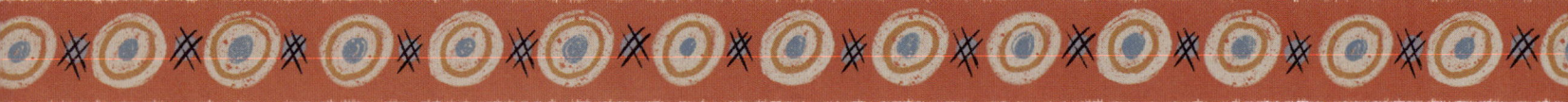

INTRODUCTION

Sitting on Egypt's Mediterranean coast, close to where the River Nile flows into the sea, lies the bustling city of Alexandria. Here, beneath the choppy waters of the city harbour, scuba divers silently comb the seabed for hidden treasure. Scattered amongst the sand and sea-life, the divers find their rewards – ancient stone sphinxes, splendid statues, barnacle-encrusted pots and beautifully carved columns. Preserved in this underwater museum, each artefact offers a tantalising glimpse of the lost world of Egypt's last pharaoh, Cleopatra VII.

Born in ancient Alexandria more than 2,000 years ago, Cleopatra's life was a whirlwind of unimaginable riches, power and glamour. But it was also bursting with danger, daring and intrigue. Glitzy parties and adoring crowds went hand in hand with murderous family feuds and all-out war. Hers was the life of a superstar, superhero and super-ruler all rolled into one – a life that saw Cleopatra become a legend long before her death at the age of just thirty-nine.

Today, the magnificent marble city that Cleopatra once called home has mostly slipped beneath the Mediterranean waves, or vanished under the buildings of modern-day Alexandria. Hardly anything remains that directly connects Cleopatra's past to our present. Yet, despite this, her remarkable story continues to captivate us. She features everywhere from films, fashion and fancy-dress shops to the planet Venus, where scientists have named a crater after her.

But although her name and her story might be familiar to us, how much do we actually know about Cleopatra herself? Are the incredible tales of her life, passed down through history, really true? And if not, what did actually happen? What is fact and what is fiction?

Let's find out by diving back in time to the dawn of ancient Alexandria, where our story begins. A true story that is more remarkable than any legend. The story of the **real** Cleopatra.

Power dressing: Cleopatra in her traditional pharaonic robes, wig and crown.

THE PTOLEMIES' EGYPT

Ancient Egypt is famous for its sun-drenched pyramids, but when Cleopatra was born in 69 BCE, these mind-boggling mega-structures were already over 2,000 years old. To put that into perspective, Cleopatra lived closer in time to the building of the first Pizza Hut than to the building of the pyramids.

In fact, Cleopatra's Egypt was quite different to the one ruled by the powerful pyramid-building pharaohs – the last of whom had died centuries before she arrived on the scene. What's more, Cleopatra wasn't actually related to any of these ancient pharaohs. She was mainly Greek, not Egyptian. Most of her ancestors were originally from the ancient Greek kingdom of Macedonia. Known as 'The Ptolemies' (pronounced toll-uh-mees), Cleopatra's family had inherited control of Egypt from the legendary Macedonian king Alexander III, better known as Alexander the Great.

A young Cleopatra pays her respects to Egyptian pharaohs of ages past.

ALEXANDER THE GREAT CONQUERS EGYPT

Born around 300 years before Cleopatra, Alexander had conquered kingdom after kingdom, creating the largest empire the ancient world had ever seen. Among the many countries he took control of was Egypt, where he ordered the construction of a glorious new city named 'Alexandria' in his honour.

Sadly, Alexander would never see his city built. Eight years after leaving Egypt, he died of a fever. His huge Macedonian empire was swiftly shared out between his generals, with Egypt going to his childhood friend, Ptolemy. So began almost three centuries of rule by fifteen successive Ptolemaic pharaohs – each called Ptolemy, and each ruling alongside their female counterpart called one of three names: Arsinoe, Berenice or Cleopatra.

THE PTOLEMIES TAKE CONTROL

The early Ptolemaic male and female pharaohs were smart rulers who created one of the most powerful and wealthy kingdoms in the world. They knew it was important to keep their Egyptian subjects happy. So, instead of forcing everyone to follow Greek traditions, they adopted important parts of Egyptian culture. Crucially, they chose to honour Egypt's powerful and ancient religious beliefs. This included allowing the Egyptian people to continue treating their rulers as gods – a tradition that had been encouraged by the ancient Egyptian pharaohs, but was alien to most Greeks.

THE POWER OF THE NILE

The success of the Ptolemaic rulers was not just down to their clever decisions though. They had been lucky enough to inherit a kingdom with a treasure trove of natural riches that were the envy of the ancient world.

Thanks to the life-giving waters of the River Nile, snaking from the south of the country to the north, Egypt's farmers produced large amounts of grain, wine, flax and papyrus, as well as a rainbow of fruits, vegetables and spices. Along with other Egyptian specialities – such as glassware and jewellery – these precious goods were traded with other countries for valuable items such as silver, timber, ivory, silk and precious stones.

But although this made them fabulously rich, the early Ptolemies were hungry for even more wealth and power. So, they fought neighbouring kingdoms and won more land, creating an empire worthy of Alexander the Great himself.

The mighty River Nile – the main source of water and life in the hot, dry deserts of ancient Egypt.

ANCIENT ALEXANDRIA: THE JEWEL IN THE PTOLEMIES' CROWN

At the heart of this empire sat the city of Alexandria, the sparkling jewel in the Ptolemies' crown. Slap bang in the centre of important trade routes, it was the ancient world's busiest and wealthiest port. But although it was the capital of Egypt, it had the appearance and feel of a Greek city.

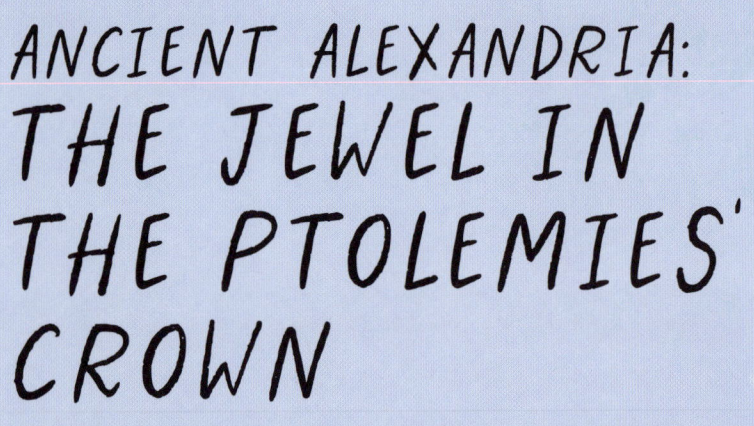

Sailors approaching Alexandria's Royal Harbour would have been greeted by the breathtaking sight of a towering, three-tiered, stone lighthouse topped by a statue of a Greek god, either Zeus or Poseidon. More than 100 metres high (taller than the Statue of Liberty), the Lighthouse of Alexandria was one of the tallest human-made structures of its time and is now known as one of the Seven Wonders of the Ancient World.

Once inside the safety of the harbour, the visiting sailors would have unloaded their cargoes at the busy wharfs – the wafts of exotic spices, briny fish and fresh fruit and vegetables filling their nostrils. With the din of merchants shouting in Greek, Egyptian, Arabic and many other tongues ringing in their ears, they would have passed beyond the crowded warehouses and the trading emporium (a large market) into the magnificent heart of the city.

Alexandria's bustling Royal Harbour hosted traders from around the world.

ALEXANDRIA

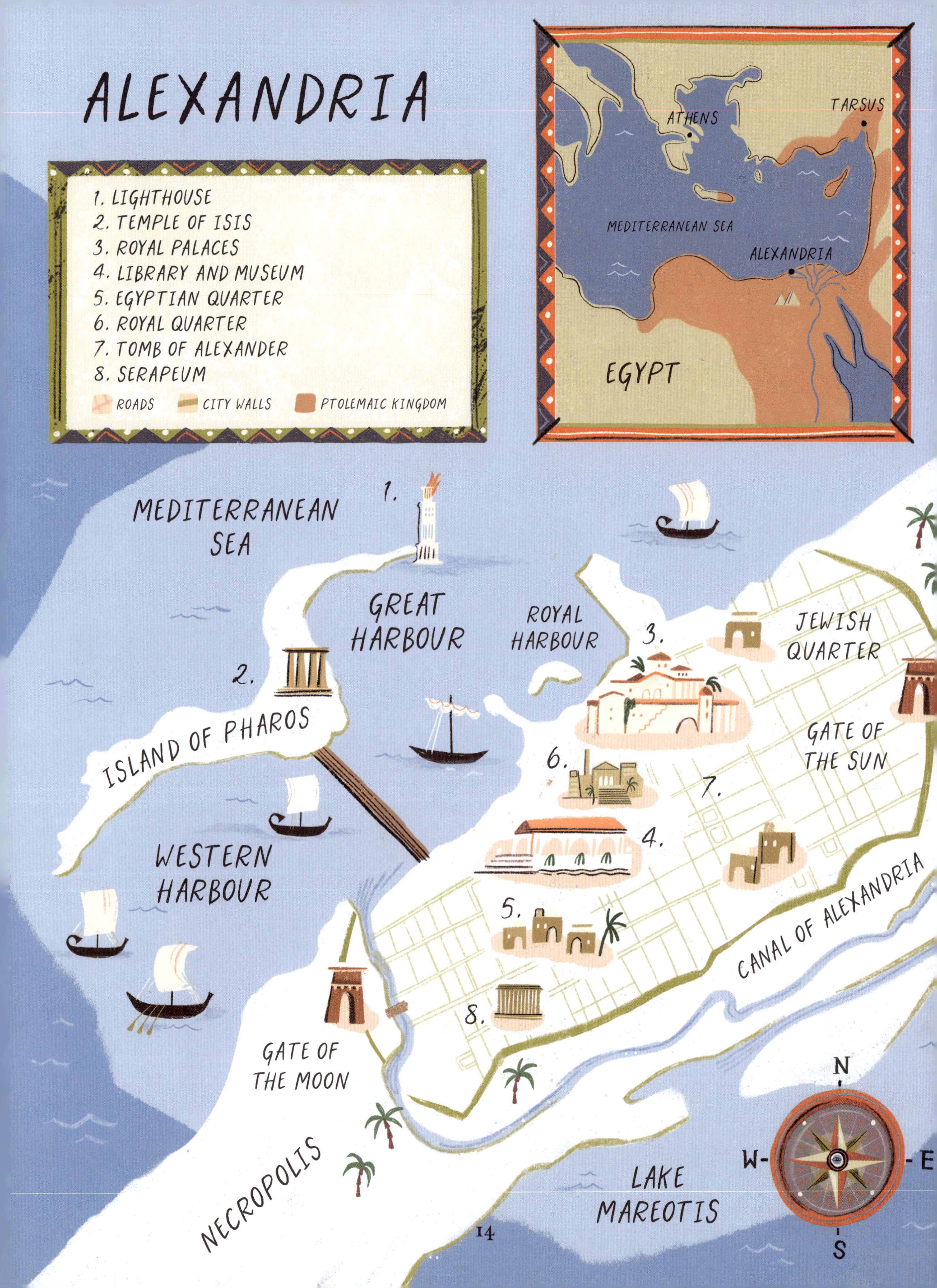

1. LIGHTHOUSE
2. TEMPLE OF ISIS
3. ROYAL PALACES
4. LIBRARY AND MUSEUM
5. EGYPTIAN QUARTER
6. ROYAL QUARTER
7. TOMB OF ALEXANDER
8. SERAPEUM

ROADS · CITY WALLS · PTOLEMAIC KINGDOM

Ancient Alexandria was famous for its wide, airy avenues lined with marble columns, majestic monuments, temples and grand buildings. The most impressive of these buildings were found in the Royal Quarter. It was here, on the breezy seafront, that the Ptolemies built their sprawling marble palaces and laid out their exotic gardens. Here also lay the tomb of Alexander the Great himself – his mummified body sealed in a glass coffin for all to see.

A short walk from Alexander's resting place sat Alexandria's legendary 'Museum', meaning 'temple to the muses'. Established by Ptolemy I and his son Ptolemy II, the Museum was not like the kind of grand building stuffed with interactive displays that you might visit today on a school trip. Instead, it was rather similar to a modern-day university. Poets, scientists, mathematicians, astronomers and philosophers – the most brilliant minds of the ancient world – travelled from near and far to live, research and share ideas there. The Museum's most prized possession was its collection of around half a million papyrus scrolls (there were no bound books, like this one, in those days). These were stored in its Great Library and were said to represent every important work that had ever been written.

So, as well as valuable goods, Alexandria also led the way when it came to trading in knowledge, learning and ideas. It was little wonder then that the Ptolemaic rulers were among the most powerful on Earth.

THE PTOLEMIES IN DECLINE

With so much power and wealth at their fingertips, it would be easy to assume that each Ptolemaic ruler would lead Egypt from strength to strength. But after an excellent start, things began to roll steadily downhill. There were two main reasons for this.

The first was that the Ptolemies had a habit of marrying within their immediate family. This meant that brothers often married sisters, and nieces wedded their uncles. The idea was to ensure that no other family had a claim to the throne. But their plan was far from foolproof. Keeping things within the family meant that, rather than fighting with others for the right to rule, the Ptolemies battled bitterly amongst themselves. Life in the royal household was brutal, with male and female rulers, and their sons and daughters, all attacking one another – often with murderous results.

All the quarrelling and back-stabbing distracted the Ptolemies from the day-to-day running of their kingdom, which began to suffer as a result. The unhappy Egyptians started rebellions, and, to make matters worse, a string of disastrous foreign wars saw Egypt lose much of its territory. Desperate to regain control of their people and recapture Egypt's former glory, the Ptolemies asked for help from an increasingly mighty neighbouring power. And this led to problem number two: the Romans.

THE RISE OF ROME

As the sun set on the golden age of the Ptolemies, it was just beginning to rise on the Roman Republic. A power-hungry state with a well-trained and much-feared army, Rome became the number one power in the Mediterranean. Egypt was a tasty target for the Roman rulers, who desperately needed Egyptian grain to feed their growing population. Amidst their family feuding, the Ptolemies had just about enough time and sense to realise that their kingdom was likely to be next on the Roman hit list, and so they went to ever greater lengths to keep the Romans as friends.

However, it soon became clear that Egypt needed Rome's friendship more than Rome needed Egypt's. Before long, Rome was regularly stepping in to help the Ptolemies fight their endless battles: with neighbouring kingdoms, with their own people and, of course, with each other. Bit by bit, a smaller and weaker Egypt began to slip under Rome's influence.

The letters SPQR, often seen on Roman banners, stood for Senatus Populusque Romanus ('The Senate and People of Rome').

By the time Cleopatra's father, Ptolemy the Twelfth (XII), came to the throne, it was a question of 'when' rather than 'if' Rome would seize control of Egypt. Ptolemy XII tried his best to avoid this by laying on the charm. He sent Egyptian soldiers to help the Romans with their conquests and paid their politicians massive bribes to leave his country alone. With the royal bank account getting emptier and emptier, Ptolemy let his people pick up the bill by raising their taxes. The Egyptians – who hated taxes almost as much as they hated Rome – now detested their own ruler even more than both of these evils put together. Alexandria – whose residents were a particularly temperamental bunch – bubbled dangerously with discontent.

A ROYAL CHILDHOOD

 afely tucked away in Alexandria's Royal Palace, the young princess Cleopatra would still have heard rumours about these unhappy rumblings.

Along with her two sisters, Berenice the Fourth (IV) and Arsinoe the Fourth (IV), and her brothers, Ptolemy the Thirteenth (XIII) and Ptolemy the Fourteenth (XIV), she lived a life of privilege and luxury. It was a life worthy of the gods themselves, which is exactly what all five children were considered to be. So, from an early age, Cleopatra had a strong belief in her own importance and total confidence in her abilities – something that would come in handy later on.

However, her confidence wasn't all down to her divine status. Cleopatra enjoyed a first-rate education, studying everything from maths, history and law, to medicine, philosophy and astronomy. What's more, she was taught by some of the smartest scholars the world had ever seen, and had access to any book she could wish for from Alexandria's Great Library.

Cleopatra was a brilliant student. Later Roman and Arab writers tell us that she was very interested in philosophy, that she understood difficult chemistry and even wrote about maths and toxicology (the study of poisons).

Cleopatra could also speak at least nine languages, making her a useful person to have around when important foreign visitors came to the palace. Astoundingly, she was the first Ptolemy in 250 years to bother learning to speak Egyptian! Up until that point, all of the Ptolemies had spoken mainly in their native Greek.

Papyrus was the chief writing material in ancient Egypt.

18

It's for this reason that many historians believe Cleopatra's mother may not have been Ptolemy XII's official wife, but possibly an Egyptian noblewoman from an important family of priests. At a time when Egyptian kings had one main wife ('the Queen') and a selection of less important ('minor') wives, it was common for royal children to have different mothers. And, even though the identity of her mother has not been found in any of the surviving historical sources, it's logical to conclude that Cleopatra was encouraged to learn the Egyptian language by an Egyptian-speaking mum.

Cleopatra practises her hieroglyphic script.

PTOLEMY XII – MUSIC AND MAYHEM

Cleopatra's father was a party-loving king, remarkable for his impressive musical skills.

On taking up the throne, Ptolemy XII, like some of his ancestors, had declared himself to be the 'new Dionysus' – the Greek god of fertility and wine. Unsurprisingly, he enjoyed hosting wild and wine-soaked fancy-dress banquets. These involved him dressing as Dionysus and serenading the partygoers with his musical pipe – which earned him the nickname 'Auletes', meaning 'flute-player' in Greek.

This kind of behaviour did not do much for his reputation as a capable ruler. Nor did it help him sort out the trouble with Rome, which reached boiling point in 58 BCE when the Romans took control of the Egyptian-ruled island of Cyprus. Furious that their king had let this happen, the Alexandrians took to the streets in protest. A petrified Ptolemy fled to Rome to hide – leaving his family behind.

Ptolemy XII enjoyed extravagant parties while he gathered high taxes from his Egyptian subjects.

We can only imagine how terrifying all this must have been for the eleven-year-old Cleopatra and her younger sister and brothers. It was not so terrifying it seems for her older sister, Berenice, who – in true Ptolemaic style – seized the chance to declare herself queen.

However, three years later – having borrowed money and troops from the Romans – a fuming Ptolemy XII marched back into Egypt to quash the uprising and reclaim his throne. Showing no mercy, he had Berenice and her supporters executed. He may have killed even more people had he not been talked out of it by a handsome twenty-eight-year-old Roman cavalry commander called Mark Antony, whom we shall meet again a little later.

Sisters, Cleopatra and Arsinoe, watch nervously as angry crowds gather outside the Royal Palace.

Back on the throne – and now heavily in debt to the Romans – Ptolemy XII needed someone to help him rule. So, in 52 BCE, he announced the appointment of a new co-ruler – the teenage Cleopatra.

TEENAGE QUEEN

Just a year after Cleopatra became her father's co-ruler, he died. Now Cleopatra was firmly on the throne, but, unfortunately, she wasn't alone.

In his will, Ptolemy XII had decreed that Cleopatra should rule Egypt alongside her ten-year-old brother, Ptolemy XIII. He also ordered that Rome should act as their 'protector', to ensure that things ran smoothly for the youngsters. Aged seventeen or eighteen, Cleopatra was far older and wiser than her immature little brother, so she did what any older sister would do in her situation – she ignored him. For eighteen months, she ruled Egypt alone, with a little help from some trusted advisors.

Ptolemy XIII and his scheming advisor, Pothinus, force Cleopatra to flee Egypt.

Wise beyond her years, Cleopatra worked hard to earn the love, respect and support of the Egyptian people. While there were a few hiccups along the way – including failed crops, countrywide food shortages and a potentially disastrous falling out with Rome – Cleopatra never lost her cool.

Meanwhile, Cleopatra's brother and his scheming advisor – an oily and ruthless man called Pothinus – had other ideas about how the country should be ruled. Furious at being pushed aside, they launched a takeover. Like her father before her, Cleopatra was forced to flee Alexandria in fear of her life.

Unlike her father, however, Cleopatra did not head for Rome. Instead, she took refuge in the Egyptian province of Palestine, where she used her powers of persuasion to raise an army. If her brother wanted the Egyptian throne, he was going to have to fight her for it.

JULIUS CAESAR
COMES TO ALEXANDRIA

As Cleopatra and her brother prepared for war against one another, across the Mediterranean Sea, Rome was bogged down in its own civil war.

A civil war is a war between citizens of the same country. Two Roman generals – Julius Caesar and Gnaeus Pompey – were battling it out to become leader of the Roman Republic. The final showdown between them took place at Pharsalus in Greece, where Caesar – with the help of his close friend, Mark Antony – crushed his opponent's forces, sending Pompey scuttling away.

Years before, Pompey had helped Cleopatra's father (the late Ptolemy XII) during his exile in Rome, giving him a place to stay and persuading other important Romans to support the desperate pharaoh's cause.

Ready to call in the favour, Pompey now asked his former friend's son, Ptolemy XIII, for help. However, the new pharaoh did not feel obliged to rescue his father's saviour. What's more, he certainly did not want the Roman civil war spilling onto Egyptian soil. So, Ptolemy turned to Pothinus – the real power behind the throne – who knew just what to do. When Pompey arrived in Egypt by boat a little while later, Pothinus had already issued his deadly orders. There was no red carpet waiting for the Roman general – just a smiling assassin with a knife. He was killed before he had even stepped onto Egyptian soil.

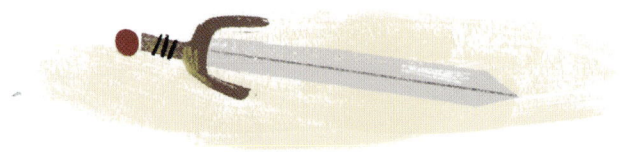

Not long afterwards, a triumphant Caesar – the newly appointed leader of Rome – arrived on the scene. As Egypt's protector, he had come to see what was going on there, and to have a go at sorting out the quarrel between its co-rulers. Above all, he wanted to lay his hands on some of the huge amounts of money that Egypt 'owed' Rome.

Arriving in Alexandria with his war ships and 4,000 soldiers, Caesar was greeted by royal officials who proudly presented him with Pompey's head. Ptolemy XIII had thought that the unusual gift would please Caesar – but he had got things badly wrong. Caesar was outraged by such brutal treatment of a fellow Roman general. Marching into the Royal Palace, he settled into his new quarters then summoned Ptolemy and Cleopatra to meet him. Solving a silly sibling squabble would be child's play for this mighty Roman general … surely?

A furious Caesar enters the Royal Palace, determined to confront the young rulers of Egypt.

CLEOPATRA AND JULIUS CAESAR

The trouble was that Ptolemy and Pothinus had no intention of letting Cleopatra anywhere near Caesar. They knew that if she charmed her way into his good books, they would lose their grip on power.

To keep her away, they posted their soldiers around Alexandria's Royal Quarter – but it would take more than that to stop Cleopatra. Abandoning her usual luxurious travel arrangements, she climbed into a small fishing boat with one of her trusted servants, Apollodorus. Undetected, the pair rowed into the Royal Harbour.

Once ashore, Cleopatra somehow avoided the attention of Ptolemy's guards and slipped into the palace to find Caesar. One legend has it that she was rolled up in a magnificent carpet and carried there by Apollodorus, who told guards that the rug was a present for Caesar. A different account has her wrapped in a large sheet, or even wearing a large cloak. However she arrived, Cleopatra's daring and determination seriously impressed the fifty-two-year-old Roman general. Caesar was immediately enthralled by Cleopatra who – with her captivating voice, brilliant brain and total self-confidence – was quite unlike anyone he had come across before.

Under the cover of darkness, Apollodorus smuggles Cleopatra into the Royal Palace.

Despite their thirty-year age gap and the tricky history between their two nations, Caesar and Cleopatra got along famously. When they appeared before a flabbergasted Ptolemy the following morning, the spark between them was blinding. Things became even worse for Ptolemy when Caesar declared that Cleopatra must return to the throne to rule alongside her brother.

This was all too much for Ptolemy. Unable to contain the rage boiling inside him, he stormed out of the palace and hurled his crown to the ground. Only a sharp word from Caesar's menacing guards persuaded the unhappy king to return inside. It was a warning of things to come. He may only have been a teenager, but he was not going to let his older sister and a Roman general get the better of him … at least not without an almighty fight.

Caesar and Cleopatra form an instant bond, much to Ptolemy's annoyance.

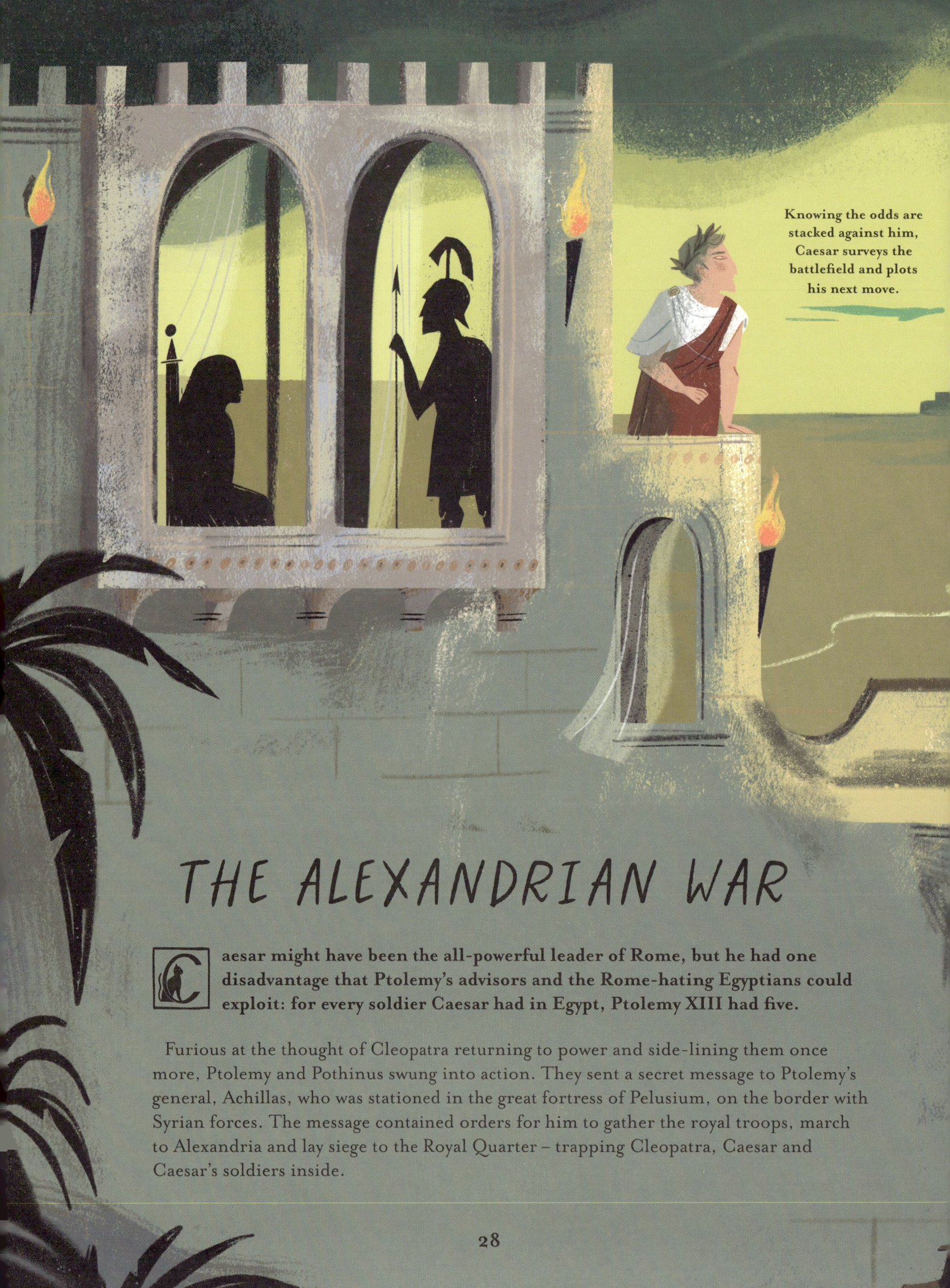

Knowing the odds are stacked against him, Caesar surveys the battlefield and plots his next move.

THE ALEXANDRIAN WAR

Caesar might have been the all-powerful leader of Rome, but he had one disadvantage that Ptolemy's advisors and the Rome-hating Egyptians could exploit: for every soldier Caesar had in Egypt, Ptolemy XIII had five.

Furious at the thought of Cleopatra returning to power and side-lining them once more, Ptolemy and Pothinus swung into action. They sent a secret message to Ptolemy's general, Achillas, who was stationed in the great fortress of Pelusium, on the border with Syrian forces. The message contained orders for him to gather the royal troops, march to Alexandria and lay siege to the Royal Quarter – trapping Cleopatra, Caesar and Caesar's soldiers inside.

As the 20,000-strong royal army approached Alexandria, Caesar sent envoys to meet them. He wanted to find out exactly what Achillas's intentions were. He didn't have to wait long. As Caesar's men entered Achillas's camp, they were attacked, and one was killed. War was just around the corner.

Back in Alexandria, Caesar wasted no time. He imprisoned Ptolemy and Pothinus inside the palace and hurriedly set up defences around the Royal Quarter and the Royal Harbour to protect himself against the advancing Egyptian soldiers. Barricaded inside, along with his 4,000 troops and the Egyptian royal family, Caesar was painfully aware how greatly outnumbered he was. To make matters worse, Achillas had the support of many thousands of armed and angry Alexandrians who were eager to banish the Romans from their city.

THE WAR CONTINUES

T he battle when it came was dirty and devastating. Achillas and his men launched attack after attack on the Royal Quarter, trying to find a way in. As well as vicious hand-to-hand fighting on the streets of Alexandria, and sea battles along the Alexandrian coastline, both sides used sneaky tactics to gain the upper hand.

The Egyptians polluted Caesar's drinking water by pumping large quantities of salty seawater into it. Meanwhile, Caesar, determined to gain control of the Great Harbour, set fire to the Egyptian fleet. As the flames spread, they engulfed a warehouse containing lots of the Great Library's priceless and irreplaceable papyrus scrolls. At one stage during the heavy fighting, Caesar's boat became overcrowded and started to sink. Ditching his famous cloak, he leapt into the harbour water and swam for his life.

Amid the confusion, Cleopatra's younger sister, Arsinoe, escaped from the Royal Quarter to join forces with Achillas.

However, things turned sour when she argued with him about what tactics to use next, and promptly had him killed.

Caesar and his men were now hanging on by the skin of their teeth – waiting for more Roman soldiers to arrive by sea. So, when the Egyptians demanded that he release Ptolemy XIII to act as a peacemaker between the two sides, Caesar agreed – to buy time. Ptolemy and Arsinoe were now declared joint rulers of Egypt by their supporters, who stepped up their efforts to destroy Caesar. But, in the nick of time, the Roman reinforcements arrived and the tables turned.

Caesar returns the captive Ptolemy XIII to Egyptian forces.

As the fighting reached a climax, Ptolemy XIII was killed – drowning in the River Nile under the weight of his heavy gold armour.

With the bloodshed finally over and her troublesome brother dead, Cleopatra was, once again, declared ruler. However, this time around, she would be ruling alongside her youngest brother – twelve-year-old Ptolemy XIV. In line with Egyptian tradition, the pair quickly married. It was not a match Cleopatra would have freely chosen – but at least her new husband would leave her in peace to govern Egypt alone.

Cleopatra with her second brother-husband, Ptolemy XIV.

A NILE CRUISE

 fter all that hard work, it was time for a holiday.

Climbing aboard her sumptuous royal yacht, Cleopatra and Caesar set off on a Nile cruise. Nothing less than a floating palace, Cleopatra's pleasure boat, with its brilliant purple sails, was ancient Egypt's equivalent to today's billionaire super-yachts. It was about the length of a football pitch, boasting two floors of gilded banqueting halls and richly decorated living spaces, a garden, shrines to the gods and stables.

As Cleopatra and Caesar relaxed on plush couches and watched the green fields of the Nile valley roll by, they were served exquisite food and entertained by musicians and performers. It was just what the doctor ordered – especially for Cleopatra, who was now pregnant with Caesar's child.

Dressed in her powerful robes and headdress, Cleopatra shows Caesar the very best of Egypt.

But, for Cleopatra, this was far more than an ancient staycation. It was a chance for her to show the Egyptian people that she was back in business – a mighty and undisputed ruler, with the gods and the most powerful man in the world on her side. It was also a chance for her to show off the very best of her famous kingdom to Caesar. As he surveyed the farmers tending their crops, gazed up at the towering Sphinx and feasted his eyes on the glorious ancient pyramids, Caesar was mightily impressed.

What's more, as he watched the high priests in their vast temples honour their divine ruler, Caesar was left in no doubt that he had backed the right sibling. Caesar could see that Cleopatra was a powerful and wise ruler. What's more, he knew he could rely upon her to run Egypt the way he needed – keeping it stable, co-operating with Rome and able to provide him with the grain he so badly needed to feed his people.

A ROYAL BABY

When the couple returned to Alexandria three months later, it was time for Caesar to go home – back to Rome, to his people and to his very understanding wife, Calpurnia. Keen to quell any further unrest amongst the Egyptians, he left four Roman legions behind to keep the peace. Cleopatra's disgraced sister, Arsinoe, went back with him – as a prisoner – to be paraded through the streets of Rome in chains. It was the very worst humiliation for a proud member of the Ptolemy dynasty, but Cleopatra shed no tears for her treacherous sibling.

Not long after Caesar had left, Cleopatra gave birth to a healthy boy. This momentous occasion was swiftly followed by another: the flooding of the Nile. For the ancient Egyptians, who depended upon the floodwater to grow their plentiful crops, this was the most important event in their calendar. It was all that stood between national feast and national famine. They were in no doubt that these two miracles of fertility were a sign that the gods were happy with Egypt and their ruler.

Cleopatra dotes on her newborn son.

Although the baby was officially called Ptolemy Caesar, the Egyptians were quick to give Cleopatra's son their own nickname – Caesarion, meaning 'little Caesar'. His proud mother, who adored her precious son beyond all else, now set about creating a powerful new identity for herself.

Just as her father had declared himself to be the 'new Dionysus', Cleopatra began to identify herself as the 'new Isis', the ancient Egyptian goddess of motherhood, fertility and magic. It was Isis, a single mother and one of the most popular gods of the day, whose tears were said to cause the yearly flooding of the Nile.

Soon, Cleopatra began dressing as Isis on important occasions – wearing a crown decorated with cobras, cow horns and a sun disc, as well as an Egyptian wig. Meanwhile, stone carvings and sculptures appeared in temples around the country depicting Cleopatra and Caesarion as the goddess and her child, Horus. Whilst the ancient Egyptians had their pick of many gods to pray to, Cleopatra actively encouraged her people to worship Isis.

This was all a very clever campaign to tighten her grip on power. By presenting herself and Caesarion as earthly versions of Isis and Horus, Cleopatra was using religion to win over the hearts and minds of her people.

After all, what human would dare question the authority of a goddess – and such an important one at that?

A giant wall carving of Cleopatra and Caesarion as Isis and Horus takes shape at the Temple of Hathor in Dendera.

A DRAMATIC VISIT TO ROME

Things were going pretty well for Cleopatra. So well in fact that just a year after Caesarion was born, Caesar invited her to visit him in Rome.

Leaving Egypt in the hands of her advisors, Cleopatra travelled to the Roman capital with her brother-husband, Ptolemy XIV, and her son. A guest of Caesar, she was showered with gifts and hosted in one of his villas.

Unsurprisingly, Cleopatra's presence caused quite a stir in the city, where gossip swirled about the exotic and powerful ruler who had enchanted their great leader. The Roman ladies – who wore plain outfits and little jewellery – were fascinated by Cleopatra's extravagant style, especially when she dressed like Isis. Her clothes, gold, jewels, make-up and pearl earrings caused envy and admiration, as well as some tut-tutting.

An exotic visitor to Rome, Cleopatra attracted a great deal of attention - both good and bad.

Meanwhile, the Roman politicians became deeply suspicious of the influence the foreign ruler held over Caesar. As a proud republic run by elected officials, the Romans had no time for kings and queens – especially not ones who claimed to be gods.

Caesar's political rivals seized the chance to spread rumours of his dastardly intentions. 'What if he overturned the Republic and declared himself King?' they asked. 'What if he declared his only son, Caesarion, to be his successor?', and, 'What if he made Alexandria his capital city, instead of Rome?'. The simmering hostility reached boiling point when Caesar boldly placed a life-sized golden statue of Cleopatra in a new temple he had built.

This was the final straw for the Roman people. On 15 March 44 BCE – known famously as the Ides of March – Caesar was stabbed to death during a meeting of the Senate (the group of politicians who ruled Rome).

While Rome reeled in shock, a desperate Cleopatra packed her bags and fled back to Alexandria. Arriving home, the full horror of what had happened hit hard. The man in whom she had invested so much – and who had saved her from her scheming brother, restored her to her throne and, above all, given her a son and heir – was dead. What's more, there was no guarantee that the next ruler of Rome would be even half as friendly and supportive towards her and her kingdom as Caesar had been. All her hard work to protect her country's independence now hung in the balance.

Yet, even amidst the turmoil, Cleopatra kept her focus and started making moves to secure her throne and her position on the world stage. Around this time, Ptolemy XIV mysteriously and rather conveniently died. Wasting no time, Cleopatra appointed her beloved four-year-old Caesarion – Caesar's only son – as her co-ruler. Egypt's fifteenth and final Ptolemy had come to the throne.

Caesar is set upon by his enemies in the Senate.

ROME:
THE STRUGGLE FOR POWER

ack in Rome, Caesar remained as divisive in death as he had been in life.

Firstly, there was the problem of his will. Many people had expected him to pass the baton of leadership on to his trusted friend and fellow general, Mark Antony. However, instead, Caesar had named his nineteen-year-old nephew, Octavian, as his heir. A fuming Antony was not going to let Octavian take charge unchallenged.

For the time being though, trouble between Antony and Octavian was put to one side due to a second, larger problem – what to do with Caesar's assassins, the two Roman senators, Marcus Junius Brutus and Gaius Cassius Longinus. Straight after Caesar's death, they had fled and were now gathering an army to march on Rome.

This threat was enough to unite Antony and Octavian – temporarily at least. Together with a third, less powerful man called Marcus Lepidus, the two rivals formed a flimsy three-way pact called the Triumvirate. Their mission: to defeat the assassins and take control of Rome once and for all.

A resentful Mark Antony looks on as Octavian addresses the people of Rome as their new leader.

Yet again, Rome prepared for civil war and, once again, Egypt looked like it would be sucked into the storm.

CLEOPATRA IN THE MIDDLE

ar is expensive, and both sides needed all the help they could get. So, Cleopatra found herself being asked for support by Brutus and Cassius on the one hand and the Triumvirate on the other.

This placed her in an impossible position. She did not particularly want to help the men who had murdered her child's father, but at the same time, she had a feeling that Octavian was no friend of hers either. After all, she had given birth to Caesar's son – an annoying reminder to Octavian that he was not Caesar's blood heir. Above all else, if she picked the wrong side, she would pay a heavy price when the victors took their revenge.

After delaying as long as she could, Cleopatra finally decided to support the Triumvirate and sent soldiers to fight Cassius in nearby Syria. Somehow though, Cassius managed to intercept her troops and get them to switch sides – an embarrassing moment for Cleopatra.

To make amends, she raised a fleet of warships and – bravely taking the helm as naval commander – set sail for Greece to help Octavian, Antony and Lepidus. However, perilous storms plagued her journey and the fleet never made it to Greece. Luckily, Cleopatra was excused from having to try again when Brutus and Cassius were finally defeated at the bloody Battle of Philippi, in what is now modern-day northern Greece.

Wasting no time, the victors divided up the Roman world between themselves. Octavian took charge of the west; Antony, the east; and Lepidus took parts of Africa and Sicily.

Clever Cleopatra had played a good game. By holding her nerve, she had won time to work out which side to back. Even better, she'd actually managed to avoid getting embroiled in any costly fighting. But, best of all, she had picked the winning team.

Now all she could do was wait and see what that team would do next.

Cleopatra's fearsome fleet of warships takes to the Mediterranean Sea.

PLOTTING THE NEXT MOVE

A triumphant Antony soon set off on a tour of his new domain. Keen to impress his people (and completely convinced of his own greatness), he did something very Egyptian in character: he appeared before them as the 'new Dionysus'. This was the same god that Cleopatra's father had claimed to be and the perfect choice for Antony, who – just like Ptolemy XII – liked nothing better than a good party.

On reaching the city of Tarsus, in the south of modern-day Turkey, Antony summoned Cleopatra to meet him. After all of her shenanigans during the recent war against Cassius and Brutus, he had some questions for her. He wanted to know if she was really loyal to the Triumvirate, and if so, what could she do to prove it?

This was a key moment for Cleopatra. If she got it right, she could win over one of the two most important men in Rome (the other was, of course, Octavian) and secure her kingdom's future. If she got it wrong, the very independence of Egypt would be at stake.

As ever, she planned her next move meticulously. Antony was a handsome forty-year-old man who enjoyed playing the hero and, lately, the god. Despite having a wife, he adored the company of women and had left a string of broken hearts across the Roman world. A woman who could play a powerful goddess to match his god would surely win his respect – if not his love.

Dionysus had long been considered the Greek version of the Egyptian god Osiris, who was Isis's dead husband. What better way to arrive for her meeting with Antony, Cleopatra calculated, than dressed as Aphrodite, the Greek version of her favourite goddess, Isis?

Dressed as Aphrodite, Cleopatra prepares to meet Mark Antony.

Cleopatra impresses Mark Antony with many lavish feasts.

LOVE AND POLITICS

One warm sunny morning in 41 BCE, a golden boat with silver oars glided up the Cydnus river, towards Tarsus. On board, serenaded by flutes and pipes, fanned by young boys dressed as Cupid, and smelling sweetly of exotic spiced perfume, Cleopatra lay under a gold-spangled canopy – a goddess on her way to meet her god.

That night, Antony asked Cleopatra to dine with him, but she refused. Instead, she invited him aboard her royal barge, where he and his friends were treated to a lavish feast that Dionysus himself would have marvelled at. At the end of the banquet, Cleopatra presented Antony with the jewel-encrusted golden plates that everyone had eaten from. Antony was enchanted and impressed – all doubts about Cleopatra's loyalty forgotten.

The feasting continued night after night, with each event more spectacular than the last. By the end of her stay in Tarsus, Cleopatra had skilfully achieved what she had set out to do. Amidst the eating, drinking and showing off, Antony and Cleopatra had actually reached a business deal. Cleopatra had agreed to help pay for a war that Antony was planning to fight against the powerful Parthian Empire. In return, Antony would protect Cleopatra's crown and her land.

To top everything off, Antony had fallen for Cleopatra hook, line and sinker, just as his friend Caesar had before him. When Cleopatra invited him to return with her to Alexandria, he jumped at the chance.

The pair spent a happy winter in Egypt's capital, feasting with friends, playing games and practical jokes and enjoying one another's company. Legend has it that, on one occasion, Cleopatra even dissolved a priceless pearl earring in a cup of strong wine and drank it to impress everyone. Antony would have stayed longer but Cleopatra reminded him gently that he had important business elsewhere. It was vital that Antony should secure his position in Rome. After all, what use would he be to her if he let Octavian steal the reins of power?

As she watched his ship leave Alexandria's Royal Harbour, Cleopatra congratulated herself on a job well done. Not only had she found herself and Egypt a new protector to replace Caesar, she was also now carrying his children – twins, who would be named Alexander Helios (Greek for 'Sun') and Cleopatra Selene (Greek for 'Moon'). With three heirs – all with powerful fathers – Cleopatra had secured the throne for generations of Ptolemies to come. Or so she thought.

ANTONY CALLS IN CLEOPATRA'S FAVOUR

Back in Rome, Antony had a few niggling problems to sort out. Although he and Octavian were meant to be allies, neither of them liked sharing power and they fought like cat and dog. Once again, civil war looked likely. Yet, neither side actually wanted to have a full-on battle. The sudden death of Antony's wife, Fulvia, presented the perfect opportunity to make something close to peace. The newly single Antony agreed to marry Octavian's sister, Octavia – a move that both sides hoped would bind them closer together and make it harder for them to fall out.

Octavian and Antony may have been brothers-in-law, but they never stopped being enemies.

However, the marriage didn't put an end to Antony's relationship with Cleopatra. In the autumn of 37 BCE, Antony summoned Cleopatra to meet him in the Greek city of Antioch. He was still set on conquering Parthia, and had decided it was time to call in the favour that Cleopatra had promised him four years earlier in Tarsus. Although Octavian had agreed to help with the campaign by providing Antony with cash and 20,000 troops, they were taking their time to arrive. In fact, Antony had a sneaking suspicion they never would. He was right to be distrustful. In truth, the pair still loathed each other, and Octavian had no desire to see his rival do well in battle. Antony now needed Cleopatra and her wealth more than ever.

This time around, however, Cleopatra was in a far stronger bargaining position – one that would help her squeeze even greater prizes out of Antony. By the end of their discussions, Cleopatra had regained control of a long list of Roman territories that had once belonged to the Ptolemaic Empire. What's more, Antony publicly acknowledged that he – one of the most powerful men in the world – was the father of Cleopatra Selene and Alexander Helios. In return for all of this, Cleopatra promised to provide Antony with ships for his navy and supplies for his troops. With their business over, the two rekindled their romance and were married in Antioch.

Mark Antony gives Cleopatra everything she asks for.

With the arrival of the spring and better weather, it was time for Antony to begin his quest. Meanwhile, a victorious Cleopatra returned to Alexandria to set about making the most of her new lands and wealth. She was also pregnant with Antony's third child – a son called Ptolemy Philadelphus (which means 'brother-loving' in Greek) who would be born later that summer.

However, watching from Rome, a wily Octavian pounced on the chance to criticise his rival. What had possessed Antony to give important bits of the Roman Empire away to a foreign ruler? And what did he think he was doing playing husband to her when he had a faithful wife – Octavian's own sister – waiting for him back at home? Angry mutterings echoed around the Senate, and the Roman public began to turn against Antony.

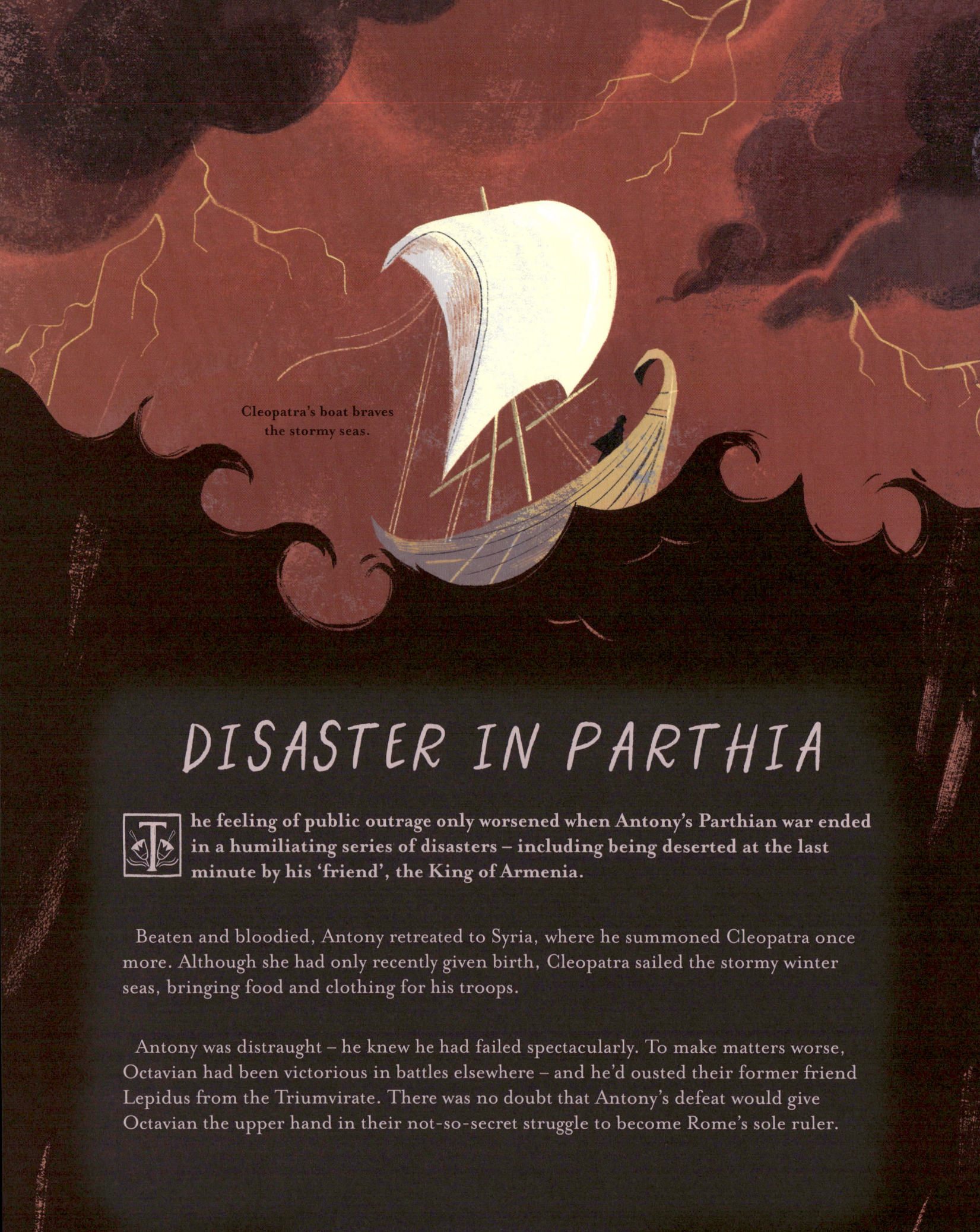

Cleopatra's boat braves the stormy seas.

DISASTER IN PARTHIA

The feeling of public outrage only worsened when Antony's Parthian war ended in a humiliating series of disasters – including being deserted at the last minute by his 'friend', the King of Armenia.

Beaten and bloodied, Antony retreated to Syria, where he summoned Cleopatra once more. Although she had only recently given birth, Cleopatra sailed the stormy winter seas, bringing food and clothing for his troops.

Antony was distraught – he knew he had failed spectacularly. To make matters worse, Octavian had been victorious in battles elsewhere – and he'd ousted their former friend Lepidus from the Triumvirate. There was no doubt that Antony's defeat would give Octavian the upper hand in their not-so-secret struggle to become Rome's sole ruler.

With Cleopatra's help and encouragement, Antony prepared to fight a second war. But – in an unexpected twist – news arrived that his wife, Octavia, was coming to meet him with 2,000 troops from Octavian. Although this looked like a friendly gesture, it was actually a trap. Octavian was offering far less help than he had originally promised, and less than Cleopatra had already provided. He had calculated that Antony would not risk upsetting Cleopatra by meeting Octavia. He also knew that when Antony chose Cleopatra over his dutiful wife, there would be uproar in Rome.

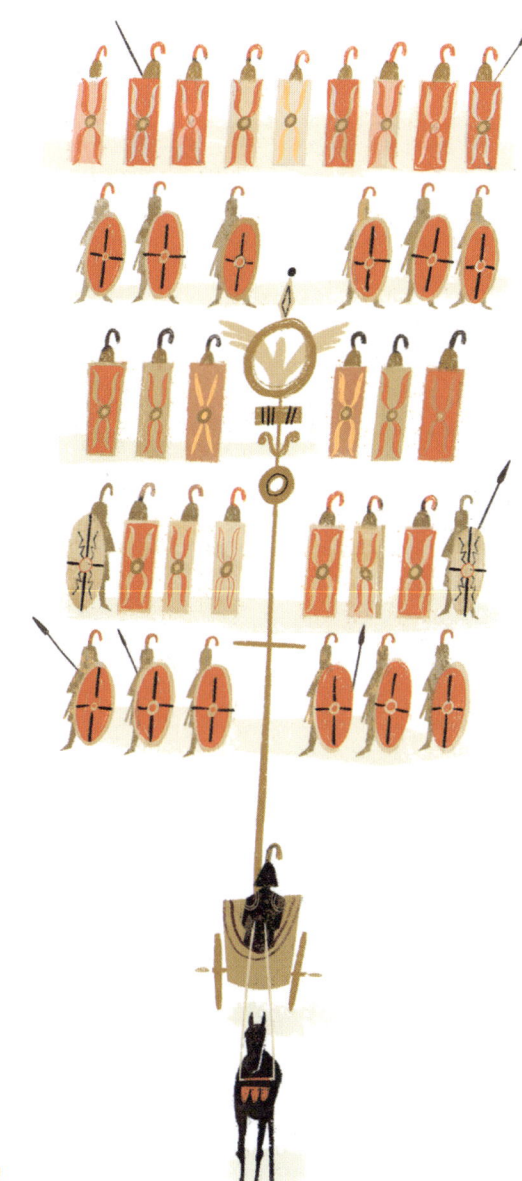

Antony's refusal to meet with Octavia was considered a great insult. He eventually divorced her in 32 BCE.

As predicted, Antony snubbed Octavia by telling her to return home. His reputation in Rome was now in tatters.

However, Antony and Cleopatra had more important things on their mind for now. In 34 BCE, Cleopatra waved Antony off to war once more. This time, he was less ambitious. Instead of trying to defeat Parthia, he made do with marching into Armenia and arresting the king in revenge for his treachery during the first Parthian war.

Cleopatra, Antony and young Caesarion – a powerful family.

THE CLOUDS OF WAR GATHER

Antony was determined to make the most of his small victory. Returning to Alexandria, he celebrated in style with a 'triumph' – a dramatic victory parade traditionally staged in Rome by Roman generals. Dressed in the golden robes of Dionysus, Antony processed through the streets of Alexandria in his chariot. Arriving at the feet of Cleopatra, who waited for him on a raised golden throne, Antony presented her with the King of Armenia and his family, bound in silver chains.

Not content with just one magnificent ceremony, Antony and Cleopatra decided to hold another. This time, they staged a huge public 'coronation', during which Cleopatra and her son Caesarion were officially crowned queen and king of the huge stretches of Roman-won territory that Antony had given to Cleopatra in Antioch. Antony then gave the three children he shared with Cleopatra their own lands to rule over, which they would inherit once they were old enough. Finally, Antony declared Caesarion to be Caesar's true son and heir.

You could almost hear the huffing and puffing in Rome. The Romans were appalled that a triumph, one of their most important and ancient ceremonies, had taken place in a foreign city, and in honour of a foreign ruler. This and the coronation were more than enough to push them over the edge. A livid Octavian raged at Anthony for all to hear. All pretence that Octavian and Antony could rule the Roman world together was abandoned. The civil war that had been brewing for so long was finally about to erupt.

While both sides gathered their armies for the final showdown, Octavian mounted a full-blown propaganda campaign against Cleopatra – spreading vicious lies about her. Rumours began to swirl about how the wicked and greedy Egyptian enchantress had bewitched Antony and tricked him into doing her bidding. It was a clever move by Octavian, who knew he would get far more support from his people if he declared war on Cleopatra, the foreign ruler, rather than Antony, the Roman hero.

Ignoring the outrageous gossip, Cleopatra busied herself with building new warships and gathering money with which to pay and equip her armies. There was no chance that she would leave Antony to lead this fight alone. This was one battle she could not let him lose – if he did, *she* would lose everything. Her fate and the fate of Egypt rested on this last roll of the dice. She was going with him.

Cleopatra readies her fleet for battle.

THE BATTLE OF ACTIUM

 he dice were rolled in the spring of 31 BCE, when the two sides met in western Greece.

Things were looking good for Cleopatra. With more troops and ships than Octavian – and with Antony's vast military experience to command them – she felt she was off to a good start. The odds and the gods were surely on her side.

But somehow, little by little, it all began to unravel. A series of poor decisions as well as some bad luck – including the exposure of their battle plans by a traitorous general – saw Antony and Cleopatra outmanoeuvred by Octavian's better-trained forces. Eventually, they found themselves pinned down in malaria-ridden marshland on the Bay of Actium. With their forces plagued by hunger, dysentery and desertions, and their warships trapped in the bay by Octavian's fleet, Antony and Cleopatra's only hope was to try and stage a break-out by sea.

Their plan was to sail straight through the menacing lines of Octavian's warships, and make a dash for Egypt where they would regroup to fight another day. It was desperate and dangerous, but it was their only chance of survival.

Battle rages in the Bay of Actium.

Finally, they made their move on 2 September 31 BCE. Early that morning, Antony and Cleopatra's large warships rowed out to face Octavian's smaller and faster fleet – led by the legendary Roman admiral, Agrippa. Octavian himself cowered from sight, feeling fragile and seasick.

After six hours of manoeuvring into place, the battle finally kicked off. Both sides attacked each other with arrows, spears and flame balls. In no time at all, the piercing blue Mediterranean sky became fogged with flames, smoke and missiles, and the fearsome sounds of roars, shouts and screams tore through the air. While Antony led from the front, Cleopatra's ship remained at the back.

Eventually, Antony's attacking line of ships began to break up, and Agrippa seized the opportunity to surround his opponents. As he did so, an eagle-eyed Cleopatra saw a gap open up in the enemy line. Immediately, she made a dash for the high seas, sailing her ship out towards Egypt – with other Egyptian vessels following on behind. In the confusion, Antony took the chance to save his own life. Abandoning his command, he leapt onto a smaller ship and sailed after her. Meanwhile, his loyal sailors, who could never have imagined their brave leader would jump ship, carried on fighting. It was a sorry moment for the once proud war hero. As he sailed towards Egypt, he sank into a deep depression.

While Antony sat silently and stared out to sea, Cleopatra began furiously plotting her next move. She knew it would not be long before Octavian and his troops were knocking on Egypt's door. But she also knew – better than most – that determination and courage could turn even the most hopeless-looking situation around. Perhaps she could still save her kingdom from Rome after all?

THE BEGINNING OF THE END

here was much to be done, and no time to lose.

For a start, it was vital that Cleopatra's people should have no inkling of the terrible defeat she had just suffered. Arriving back in Alexandria, she ordered her ships to be decked with garlands and victory flags. Musicians played triumphant songs in praise of the great queen as she disembarked at the Royal Harbour. So far, so good.

Next, she began preparing for the invasion that would surely come. Most importantly, she moved all of her treasure to her specially built fortress-like tomb in the city. Nestling it amongst flammable material, she planned to use it as a bargaining chip. If Octavian made a false move, she would set it alight – along with herself. This would be disastrous for the Roman leader, who desperately needed her wealth to pay his increasingly disgruntled troops.

Cleopatra gazes at her treasures for what might be the last time.

Cleopatra hoped, however, that it would not come to this. Perhaps Octavian would listen to reason? Maybe he would compromise? He might even let Caesarion rule Egypt if she stepped down? In an attempt to hold off the invasion, she entered into a series of long-distance negotiations with the Roman ruler. Octavian, however, made no promises and gave no ground.

Despite Cleopatra's best efforts to put on a brave face, nothing could disguise the horrible truth that these were the desperate last days of a doomed kingdom. Octavian's armies were on the move and closing in from all sides. Cleopatra and Antony were trapped in a gilded prison – there was nothing to do but wait.

Finally, in the summer of 30 BCE, Octavian and his troops arrived on the outskirts of Alexandria. At sunrise on 1 August, Antony and Cleopatra waved goodbye to one another. As he rode off towards the enemy lines, there was little doubt that this was a battle even the mighty Antony could not win.

Although Antony was prepared to throw everything he had into this last desperate fight, his forces had other plans. Realising that defeat was inevitable, they surrendered to the other side before the first arrows had even been fired.

A humiliated Antony retreated to the Royal Palace to await his fate with his queen. However, on arriving home, he discovered that Cleopatra had already fled to her tomb with her maids, Charmion and Eiras. Believing she had gone ahead with her plan to kill herself, and knowing there was now nothing left to live for, Antony stabbed himself in the stomach with his own sword. Teetering on the verge of death, he was carried to Cleopatra's tomb, where he died in her arms.

A distraught Antony prepares for death.

CLEOPATRA HAS THE FINAL WORD

 **ntony was now at peace, but he had unknowingly left Cleopatra at the mercy of Egypt's new conqueror.**

In fact, Octavian's men were already on their way to find her. Desperate to stop her from destroying herself and her treasure, Octavian had ordered Cleopatra be removed from her tomb. While one soldier distracted her with a conversation – held through a tiny crack between the door and the wall – another managed to climb up a ladder and in through a high window. Realising what was happening, Cleopatra reached for her dagger, intending to kill herself. But it was too late, the weapon was seized from her grasp and she was escorted back to the Royal Palace under armed guard.

Imprisoned in her own palace, Cleopatra was convinced she would be taken to Rome and paraded through the streets in chains – just as her sister, Arsinoe, had been 16 years earlier. With this at the forefront of her tortured mind, the defiant ruler planned her final triumph over Rome. On 12 August, she asked to visit Antony's tomb to offer him her prayers. On returning to the palace afterwards, she bathed and dressed in her royal robes before sitting down to a feast that ended with a basket of juicy purple figs. Once she had eaten her fill, she sent a sealed message to Octavian asking that she be buried alongside Antony. Then she closed the doors to her chamber for the final time.

Having read her message, Octavian hurriedly dispatched his servants to find out just what was going on. Arriving at Cleopatra's door, they discovered the guards standing outside and no sign of trouble. But on entering the room they were aghast to see a serene and splendid Cleopatra lying lifeless on her golden couch. Meanwhile, her faithful maids, Charmion and Eiras lay dying at her feet. The last ruler of Egypt had

OCTAVIAN'S TRIUMPH OVER EGYPT

Whilst some say that Cleopatra died from the bite of a poisonous snake hidden in the basket of figs, others say that she injected herself with poison concealed in a hairpin. Yet with no witnesses and no crime scene, the truth of how Cleopatra died is yet another secret that she took to her grave.

However it was that she killed herself, one thing is for certain: her death at the age of thirty-nine marked the end of ancient Egypt's independence. At the end of August 30 BCE, Octavian formally took control of the once proud and mighty kingdom of Egypt. It was now just another cog in the mighty Roman machine.

Intent on keeping it that way, Octavian showed no mercy to sixteen-year-old Caesarion, killing him as soon as he got the chance. Cleopatra and Antony's three children, however, were quickly shipped off to Rome. The two boys were never heard of again, while Cleopatra's daughter was cared for by Antony's long-suffering former wife, Octavia.

As for Octavian, with no rival to challenge him, it was not long before he had dissolved the Roman Republic. Reinventing himself as 'Caesar Augustus', he became Rome's first emperor and even renamed the month of August after himself in celebration of his victory over Cleopatra. Over the next forty years, Octavian brought peace and stability to the Mediterranean and was eventually proclaimed a god on his death in 14 CE. As an emperor and a god, he was everything that Brutus and Cassius had feared Caesar would become.

Laying down the law: Cleopatra gives orders to her officials.

THE REAL CLEOPATRA

It is often said that history is written by the victors – and in Cleopatra's case this is certainly true. Following her death, Octavian carried on doing all he could to paint Egypt's last ruler in a bad light, and himself as the conquering hero. The smears stuck, and in the centuries since her death she has been depicted in art, films and on paper as a beautiful temptress, an extravagant party girl and a ruthless baddie.

Even today, despite historians' efforts to sort fact from fiction, we still focus on those fabled parts of Cleopatra's life that may or may not be true – her bewitching beauty, her escapade in an exotic carpet, her pearl-drinking and her death by snakebite.

But if we look a little more closely, we can see that beyond these colourful stories lies a much more remarkable tale. The tale of a woman who, in a world dominated by men, became one of the most powerful rulers of her day. The tale of a leader and a survivor who spoke many languages, wrote books, commanded a navy and steered her country carefully through hunger, debt and civil war. The tale of a ruler who, against the odds, very nearly saved her kingdom from the mighty power that was Rome. The tale of the real Cleopatra.

TIMELINE

BCE

331: Alexander the Great founds Alexandria

323: Alexander the Great dies

305: Alexander the Great's general, Ptolemy, declares himself King Ptolemy I of Egypt

170–116: Rome's influence over Egypt increases during the reign of Ptolemy VIII

43: Octavian, Mark Antony and Lepidus form the Triumvirate

46: Cleopatra visits Rome

44: Caesar is assassinated by Brutus, Cassius and other Roman senators

Octavian (later called 'Caesar Augustus') is declared Caesar's heir

Ptolemy XIV dies

Caesarion becomes co-ruler of Egypt with Cleopatra

41: Cleopatra sails to Tarsus to meet Mark Antony

37: Cleopatra joins Mark Antony in Antioch, Syria

42: Brutus and Cassius are defeated at Philippi, Greece. Both men die, with Brutus's death signalling the victory of the Triumvirate

40: Mark Antony marries Octavia, sister of Octavian

Cleopatra gives birth to twins by Mark Antony: Alexander Helios and Cleopatra Selene II

c.69: Birth of Cleopatra VII Thea Philopater (Cleopatra)

51: Ptolemy XII dies. Cleopatra rules Egypt with her younger brother, Ptolemy XIII, as co-ruler

80: Cleopatra's father, Ptolemy XII (Auletes), becomes king of Egypt

52: Cleopatra becomes co-ruler of Egypt with her father

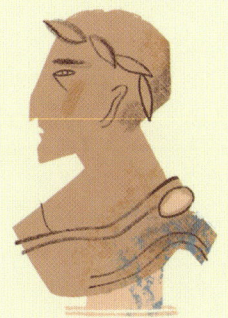

48-47: Julius Caesar helps Cleopatra during the Alexandrian War against Ptolomy XIII

48: Cleopatra flees to Palestine

47: Ptolemy XIII dies. Ptolemy XIV becomes co-ruler of Egypt with Cleopatra

Cleopatra gives birth to Caesar's son, Ptolemy XV Caesar (Caesarion)

48: Julius Caesar defeats Pompey at Pharsalus

Pompey is assassinated under the orders of Ptolemy XIII

34: Mark Antony invades Armenia

Mark Antony and Cleopatra hold a spectacular 'triumph' (victory parade) and coronation in Alexandria

30: Mark Antony and Cleopatra die. Caesarion dies shortly after

Octavian takes control and Egypt becomes part of the Roman Empire

36: Mark Antony attacks Parthia

Cleopatra gives birth to Mark Antony's son, Ptolemy Philadelphus

31: Battle of Actium

CE 14: Octavian dies

GODS IN CLEOPATRA'S EGYPT

The ancient Egyptians worshipped over a thousand gods and goddesses. People could pretty much pick and choose which ones they wanted to worship!

Each god, or deity, represented something different – from the sky and the sun to linen, beetles and centipedes! Some deities were more important than others and, over the course of ancient Egyptian history, various gods went in and out of fashion. When the Ptolemies came to power, they introduced Greek versions of Egyptian gods into the mix.

Here are some of the most important gods in Cleopatra's Egypt:

Isis: The goddess of motherhood, fertility and magic
She was the mother of the god Horus. The Greeks saw her as the Egyptian version of their goddess, Aphrodite.

Osiris: The god of the dead and ruler of the underworld, also the god of resurrection and fertility
Osiris was the brother and husband of Isis and the father of Horus. The Greeks saw Osiris as the Egyptian version of Dionysus, the Greek god of fertility and wine.

Horus: The god of kingship and the son of Isis and Osiris
The Egyptians believed that Isis and Horus were the perfect example of mother and child. This is why Cleopatra encouraged Egyptians to view her as the living Isis and her son, Caesarion, as the living Horus.

Ra: The god of the Sun
As the most important of Egypt's ancient gods, Ra could take many forms and was believed to have created all life.

Poseidon: The Greek god of the sea
A grand temple, known as the Poseidion, was built in Alexandria in his honour.

Zeus: King of the ancient Greek gods and god of the sky and thunder
Scholars think that the statue at the top of the Lighthouse of Alexandria was a depiction of either Zeus or Poseidon.

Serapis: A fusion of several Greek and Egyptian gods
The Ptolemies hoped the worship of Serapis would unite everyone in their empire, and although he was hugely popular in Alexandria with its great Serapis temple, he was never popular with native Egyptians.

GLOSSARY

Artefact a human-made object that is studied to learn more about history

Astronomer someone who studies objects in the sky (including stars, planets and galaxies)

Cavalry soldiers who fought on horses

Civil War a war between two groups of people living in the same country

Dysentery an infection that causes diarrhoea, stomach cramps and vomiting

Empire a group of countries ruled by a single person, government or country

Envoy someone who belongs to one group or government and delivers messages to another

Fleet a group of ships that sail together, often to war

Gilded something that is covered in gold

Heir the person who is next in line to the throne

Hieroglyphics a writing system that uses pictures and symbols instead of letters and words

Ivory the material that makes up tusks of animals such as elephants, often used in the past to make ornaments

Malaria an often deadly infection, spread by mosquitoes

Merchant someone who buys and sells goods, often travelling to other countries

Philosopher someone who explores big questions about life and the universe

Republic a type of government in which people elect their leaders

Sphinx a mythical creature with the head of a human and the body of a lion – ancient Egyptians believed the sphinx was a guardian figure

Siege when armed forces surround a city or building in order to try to take control of it

Taxes money that people have to pay to the government

Wharf a place where ships moor to unload cargo